More Book Factory

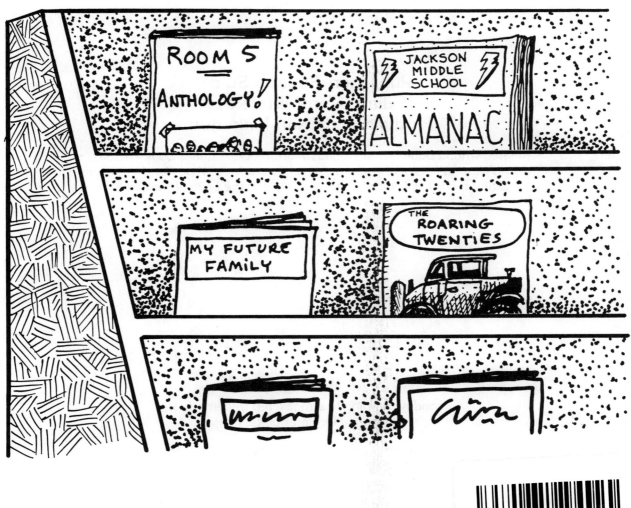

by Murray Suid and Wanda Lincoln • illustrated by Mike Artell

Publisher: Roberta Suid
Editor: Carol Whiteley
Production: Susan Pinkerton

Related writing books from Monday Morning Books, Inc: *Book Factory, Writing Hangups, Greeting Cards, Write Through the Year, For the Love of Editing, For the Love of Letter Writing, For the Love of Research, For the Love of Stories.*

ISBN 1-878279-18-1

Printed in the United States of America
9 8 7 6 5 4

For a complete catalog, write to the address above.

CONTENTS

INTRODUCTION

There's a simple but powerful way to nurture literacy: Teach students to create their own books. Helping them to produce—as well as consume—knowledge is the key to the process known as **whole learning.**

This is what *More Book Factory* is all about. Here, you will find ideas for creating atlases, diaries, historical novels, travel guides, and dozens of other works of the sort found in any good library or book shop. These varied projects make it clear that writing is important throughout the curriculum.

METHODS AND MODELS

Each lesson features specific steps that will help young authors—working alone or cooperatively—to produce fun-to-read and valuable books. The materials can be duplicated and used directly by older children or they can be adapted for younger children.

But directions are not the whole story. For truly effective learning, students need to read and study models. By sharing published almanacs, autobiographies, how-to guides, and other publications, you will sharpen students' writing skills while broadening their interest in reading—especially in reading nonfiction. (See Book List.)

BONUS PAGES

The book includes two bonus resource sections. The first, "Creating a Classroom Publishing Company," outlines strategies for setting up a classroom publishing company. Involving students in such an activity can prove highly motivating as students learn to meet their own needs and those of the entire school community. Here's a chance to teach responsibility, work habits, and the writing process.

The second bonus, "Desktop Publishing Comes to School," gives simple tips for using the modern technology of desktop publishing with children.

Happy publishing!

ABC BOOK FOR BIG KIDS

Most ABC books are for little children. But with a twist big kids can enjoy their ABCs, too. The ABC book is modeled on *Q Is for Duck.*

DIRECTIONS:
1. Choose a subject for an ABC book—sports, animals, TV, geography, whatever.
2. Brainstorm as many words and phrases as possible that relate to the subject. For example, football words might include *halfback, kick, pass, tackle,* and *touchdown.*
3. Pick one of the words or phrases, for example, *kick.*
4. Relate that word to a word that starts with a different letter, for example, *foot.*
5. Write a line that shows what *foot* has to do with *kick:*
   F is for kick. Why? Because you kick with your FOOT.
6. Use the same pattern for each letter of the alphabet:
   A is for halfback. Why? Because a halfback zooms toward the goal line like an ARROW.
   B is for tackle. Why? Because a tackle usually is a BIG player.
7. Draw a picture for each clue.
8. When making the actual pages, put the "Because" part of the riddle on the following page. This way the reader will have a chance to guess the reason before reading it.

A Sample ABC Book: ABC at Home

A is for roof. Why? Because the ANTENNA for the TV is up there.

B is for refrigerator. Why? Because that's where BUTTER is kept.

C is for freezer. Why? Because it keeps food COLD.

D is for radio. Why? Because we DANCE to the music.

E is for stereo system. Why? Because you listen to it with your EARS.

F is for wall. Why? Because a picture in a FRAME hangs on it.

G is for bathtub. Why? Because water GURGLES down the drain.

H is for faucet. Why? Because HOT water comes out.

I is for gutter. Why? Because ICICLES hang from it.

J is for shelf. Why? Because JARS sit on it.

K is for lock. Why? Because you need a KEY to open it.

L is for soap. Why? Because it makes LATHER.

M is for bathroom. Why? Because that's where you can find a MIRROR.

N is for yard. Why? Because that's where you can see a bird's NEST.

O is for door. Why? Because it leads you OUTSIDE.

P is for dining room. Why? Because PLATES are used there.

Q is for microwave. Why? Because it heats food QUICKLY.

R is for window. Why? Because you RAISE it to let in air.

S is for driveway. Why? Because you can SWEEP it.

T is for attic. Why? Because it's at the TOP of the house.

U is for drawer. Why? Because UNDERWEAR is kept there.

V is for porch. Why? Because when you sit on it, you have a VIEW.

W is for TV. Why? Because we WATCH it when our homework is done.

X is for silverware. Why? Because there's an EXTRA spoon.

Y is for fence. Why? Because it encloses the YARD to keep in the dog.

Z is for toy chest. Why? Because it contains a model ZOO.

ADVICE BOOK

Life is filled with little problems: A meatball falls into a person's lap. Or someone's dog chases a neighbor's cat up a tree. Everyone wants to know what to do when these things happen. That's why advice books are popular.

DIRECTIONS:

1. List problems that need solutions. The problems can come from everyday life, for example, how to handle a bully. Or they can be unusual, for example, what to say when greeting people from a flying saucer. *Hint:* Try collecting problems from friends, neighbors, or family members.

2. Decide whose name will appear as the answer giver. It could be the real name of the writer. Or it could be a made-up expert, for example, "Smarty Pants."

3. For each page of the advice book, pick one problem and describe it in a letter:

> Dear Smarty Pants,
>
>   Each year for my birthday my aunt gives me a tie. I hate ties. Should I tell her?
>
>   T. G.

4. Think up a good answer for each problem.

5. Copy the problem and the advice onto a page.

Variation: Write an advice book for storybook characters such as the Big Bad Wolf, Cinderella, or the Three Little Pigs.

Sample Topics for Advice Books

Everyday activities to write an advice book for:

What to say to a door-to-door salesperson

What to do when you fail a test

What to say after forgetting someone's birthday

What to do when you lose your house key

What to say when you buy something at a store but find out you've left your money at home

How to tell someone at the table that a piece of food is stuck to his or her chin

What to say when you've dialed a wrong number

How to treat the other team when your team wins the game

What to say when you meet someone who knows you but you can't remember the person's name

What to write when you are answering a letter after a year has gone by

What to say when you have forgotten to do a chore that you promised to do

Storybook characters to write an advice book for:

Troll in *The Three Billy Goats Gruff*

Three Little Pigs

Big Bad Wolf

Three Bears

Goldilocks

Cinderella

Cinderella's stepsisters

Rumpelstiltskin

Snow White

ALMANAC

Most almanacs answer questions such as "How far is it from the Earth to the moon?" or "Where is the coldest spot in the world?" What's needed is an almanac with interesting information about a place close to home.

DIRECTIONS:

1. Choose the place that the almanac will cover. It could be home, school, the neighborhood, or town.

2. List lots of questions that can be answered with facts. For example, a home almanac with a section on distances might answer questions such as "How many steps are there from the front door to the refrigerator?"

3. Get the information. In some cases, facts can be gathered firsthand, for example, by pacing off distances. In other cases, facts will come from people or books.

4. Present the facts in paragraphs. Or arrange them in chart form.

5. Add an index. It's an alphabetical list that tells readers which page will have each kind of information.

Categories for a School Almanac

Climate
    average daily temperature
    coolest place
    hottest place

Distances between places in the school

Expenses
    electricity
    heating
    water

Library
    number of books in collection
    most popular author
    number of books lost each year
    number of books added each year
    number of books circulated each year

Raw materials
    number of pencils/crayons used each year
    amount of writing paper used each year
    amount of toilet paper consumed each year

Student facts
    number of boys/girls
    number of students at each grade level
    future job goals
    favorite and least favorite subjects

Teacher facts
    number of years teaching
    college attended
    hobbies

ANTHOLOGY

An anthology is a collection of writing, usually by many authors. It can focus on one type of writing, for example, just haiku or just short stories. Or the anthology can mix together many kinds of writing.

DIRECTIONS:
1. Decide what kind of anthology to make. If the anthology will have just one kind of writing, what will it be? If it's going to be a mixed anthology, list the different kinds of writing to include.
2. Make a sketch of how all the pages should look. Each page might include a title, an illustration, and a few words about the author.
3. Ask people to contribute to the anthology. Be sure to tell them about what each page will look like. Also, give them a deadline—a date by which the writing must be finished. Invite each author to illustrate the page or have someone else do the art.
4. When putting the book together, include a contents page. List each title and the writer's name.
5. If possible, make a copy for each person who created something for the anthology.

ART BOOK

A picture can tell a story all by itself. But adding a few words to the picture can make the story even better.

DIRECTIONS:

1. Decide what kind of art to include. Will all the art be by one artist? Or will the book contain art by many people? Also, will the art have just one subject, for example, animals—or will the pictures be about many different things?

2. Create or collect the pictures. These can be original art or pictures from post cards or from magazines.

3. Write a short caption—a few sentences or paragraphs—for each picture. Because readers can see for themselves, the words should not describe the picture. Instead, a caption might explain why the artist created the picture. Or it might say something that will make the viewer look at the picture in a new way.

4. Mount each picture and its caption on a sheet of paper.

OUR CLASS WENT ON A DRAWING FIELD TRIP.

ATLAS

An atlas is a bound collection of maps. A world atlas contains maps of Canada, France, Italy, the United States, and so on. A personal atlas contains maps of places from a person's everyday life.

DIRECTIONS:
1. Make a list of familiar places. This might include rooms at home, places at school, a friend's house, the dentist's office, the playground, even places read about or seen on TV.
2. For each place, draw a bird's-eye picture that includes all important details.
3. Give each map a title.
4. Add a few lines to explain why the place is important.
5. Make a table of contents that lists the maps in the atlas.

Variation: Create an atlas of imaginary places told about in books, comics, movies, and TV shows, for example, Alice's Wonderland, the Land of Oz, the world of Narnia.

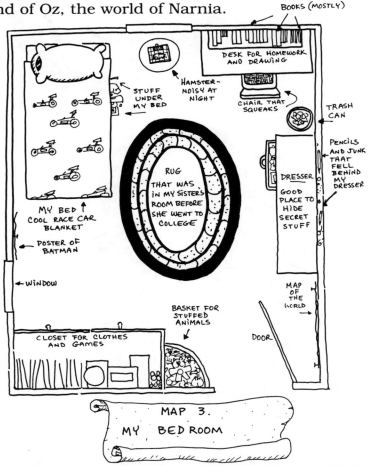

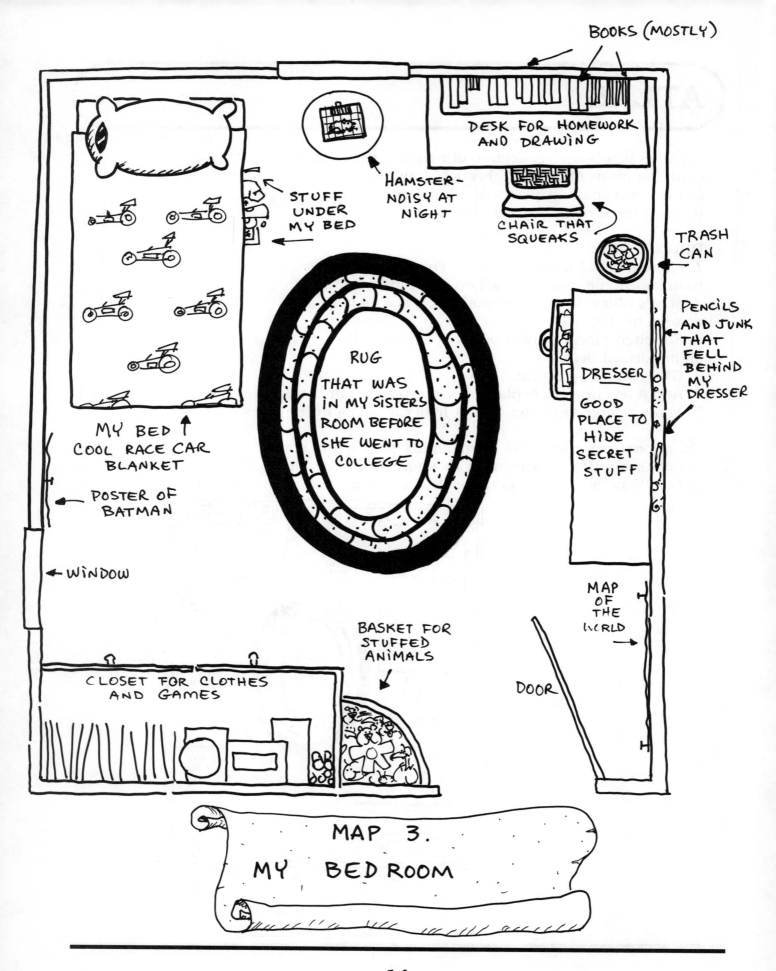

AUTOBIOGRAPHY

An autobiography is the story of a person's life written by that person.

DIRECTIONS:
1. Figure out how much of your story to tell. Will it cover your entire life or just feature a few years? Will it include facts about many activities or will it focus on a few very important ones such as music or athletics or a hobby?
2. Collect plenty of facts and stories. For example, an autobiography about becoming a saxophone player might include facts about practicing, concerts, favorite music, and other musicians in the family.
3. Write the story. Add interesting photos or drawings.
4. Write an introduction that gives readers a hint about what makes this life story worth learning about.

Variation: Write a fictional autobiography about someone or something that cannot write. It might be the "autobiography" of a baby in the family, a pet goldfish, or the "autobiography" of a bicycle.

BEST OF ITS KIND

It's fun to read about the things people love, and even more fun to write about favorites.

DIRECTIONS:
1. Make a list of categories of things: books, cars, cartoon characters, family activities, food, heroes, hobbies, movies, places, restaurants, school subjects, songs, sports, TV shows, toys.
2. Pick one favorite for each category. The selection can be made by one person, for example, "Sandy's Favorites"—or it can be the decision of a group.
3. Draw each favorite and write a few lines or a paragraph explaining why it is so special.
4. Collect the favorites in a book with a title that tells the reader that there is news inside about terrific things.

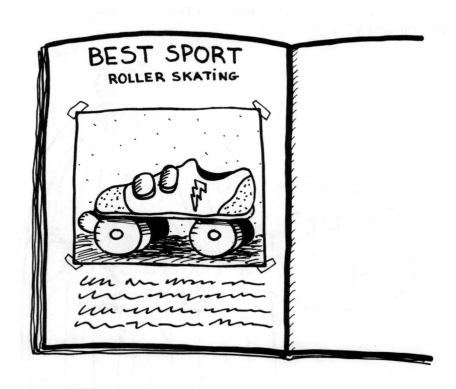

CAR-RIDING FUN BOOK

The average person spends many hours each year riding in cars. No wonder drivers and passengers get bored! If only someone told them how to enjoy that time.

DIRECTIONS:
1. Decide whom the book is for—little children? elementary students? teenagers? families?
2. List—maybe with the help of friends—activities that can be done while traveling in a car: word games, observation games (like spotting objects in alphabetical order), songs, and so on.
3. Describe each activity on its own page. Add pictures as needed.
4. Write an introduction that explains what the book is about and why people should read it.

EDOC KOOB (= CODE BOOK)

Yhw tel seips evah lla eht nuf fo gnikam sedoc?

DIRECTIONS:

1. Invent a few different kinds of codes. For each one, include the key to the code—how to write it. Also include a sample message. *Hint:* To get ideas about making up codes, read a code book or an article about codes in the encyclopedia.

2. Write an introduction that explains several ways codes can be used, for example, in letters to friends or in a private diary.

3. To add interest, write a chapter that gives the history of codes.

Five Simple Kinds of Codes

1. Word Reversed Code: Write each word backwards. For example:

Regular words	Coded words
She smiles.	Ehs selims.

2. Letter Substitution: Pair each letter of the alphabet with a different, randomly chosen letter. For example:

Regular letters	Code letters
a	g
b	r
c	m

Sample word: cab   Coded word: mgr

3. Number Substitution: Pair each letter of the alphabet with a different number. For example:

Letters	Code numbers
a	1
b	4
c	7

Sample word: cab   Coded word: 714

4. Letter and Number Substitution: Use both letters and numbers in the code. For example:

Regular letters	Code letters/numbers
a	1
b	g
c	4

Sample word: cab   Coded word: 41g

5. Special Subject Dictionary: Substitute new words for old words.

Old words	New words
baseball	water
hit	write
home run	blue
pitch	chair

Coded message: *When you chaired me the water, I wrote a blue.*

COLLECTION BOOK

What's junk to one person may be a treasure to someone else. But with a little explanation, everyone can understand what makes an item worth collecting.

DIRECTIONS:
1. Find someone who collects a certain kind of thing—autographs, baseball cards, bottle caps, buttons, chairs, chess sets, coins, dishes, dolls, license plates, magazine covers, matchbooks, model airplanes, old radios, post cards, rare photographs, records, stuffed animals, whatever.
2. Talk to the collector. Find out interesting facts about the items.
3. Choose a dozen or so items to write about. Look for those that are especially unusual, valuable, beautiful, or just plain interesting.
4. Along with the writing, draw each item and add words that explain what makes it special.
5. Write an introduction that describes the whole collection and tells why the person likes collecting that particular thing. Include information about how other people might start their own collections.

COMICS WITHOUT DRAWING

Some of the most popular heroes of all time are found in comics. These include Lucy and Charlie Brown, Calvin and Hobbs, and Superman. While most creators of comics know how to draw, here's a way for people who aren't artists to make comics.

DIRECTIONS:
1. Collect a pile of unwanted comic strips. They can be just one kind, for example, Donald Duck—or a mixture.
2. Cut out pieces of plain white paper to cover up the dialogue balloons—the shapes that hold the words the characters speak.
3. Glue the white paper over the dialogue balloons.
4. Think up new words for the characters to say. The words should make a completely new joke or story out of the comic.
5. Use scratch paper to figure out just which words to use. Then write the words in the balloons.
6. Paste each re-done comic strip onto paper and bind into a comic-strip collection.

Variation: Use the same method to rewrite an entire comic book.

COOKBOOK

Cookbooks aren't just for cooking. They also can be for reading.

DIRECTIONS:
1. Make a list of favorite foods. The list can include foods for breakfast, lunch, dinner, snacks, picnics, and parties.
2. On separate pages, give directions for preparing each food that will be included in the cookbook. The directions can come from other cookbooks or from expert cooks.
3. As an extra treat, include facts or poems or stories about each food. For example, a page about making an ice cream sundae could include the history of the sundae. A page about making pickles could tell a true story about the time a jar of pickles spilled in the family car.
4. Illustrate each page with art that shows how to make the food or that goes with the "extra" writing.

DIARY

Each day in a person's life is valuable. Keeping a diary is one way to remember this important truth.

DIRECTIONS:
1. Bind a blank book with enough pages for at least a month of writing. Add borders and special art on the cover.
2. On the first page of the blank diary, list the kinds of activities to record: for example, chores, people met, places visited, jobs finished, books read, movies seen, ideas thought about, dreams dreamed, plans made, troubles encountered, problems solved.
3. Pick a regular time to write in the diary. Be sure to date each entry.
4. To keep the writing private, invent code words for people's names or an entire code for all the writing. (One famous writer's diary code was not broken for hundreds of years.)

Variation: Create a diary for an imaginary character, for example, a visitor from another planet or the hero of a movie.

DICTIONARY OF MANY MEANINGS

Most words can mean more than one thing. An example is pen—something to write with and something to keep a pig in. Learning to notice these multiple meanings is important in both reading and writing.

DIRECTIONS:
1. List words that have two or more meanings. *Hint:* For ideas, look through a dictionary or ask friends to suggest examples.
2. On each page of the book, explain different meanings of one word. For example, on a page labeled "Pluto," explain that Pluto is a character in a Disney cartoon and also the name of a planet. Try to write one sentence that uses the word in both ways, for example: "I wouldn't want to visit the planet Pluto just to see a Pluto cartoon."
3. Write an introduction that tells how to find a word's different meanings in a dictionary.

Variation: Write an entire book that shows the different meanings of one word. Examples of words with dozens of meanings are *go, run,* and *sit.*

Words with Two or More Meanings

bark

bill

cover

eye

fly

glass

hit

jam

Jupiter

light

marble

match

nail

out

seal

slide

snap

stamp

star

swing

tire

watch

well

FAMILY FUTURE

Some people can trace their family trees back hundreds of years, to great-great-great-great-great-great (and more great) grandparents. But this project goes in the other direction—into the future.

DIRECTIONS:

1. Make an imaginary family tree of future relatives. It will show children and grandchildren who will be living in the twenty-first century or beyond.

2. Write a story about the life of one person from the future. Include facts about the person's education, work, home, hobbies, and achievements. Be imaginative. Perhaps this future relative will live on the moon and take vacations on Mars.

3. Bind the story about the future relative and the family future tree into a book.

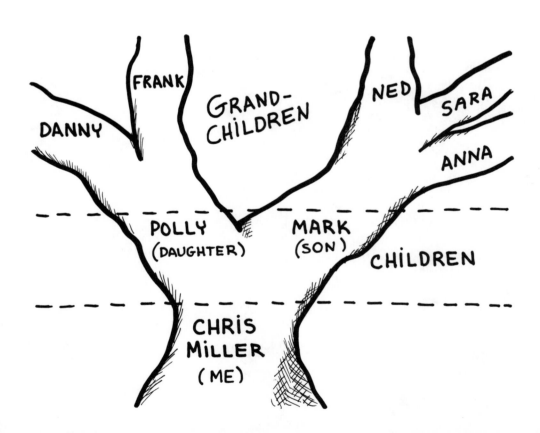

FIX-IT BOOK

Buying new things to replace old ones is easy. But it may be cheaper —and more creative—to make repairs.

DIRECTIONS:
1. List things that sooner or later need repair.
2. Figure out how each thing can be fixed. This may require asking an expert for some tips. For example, a librarian can give advice on mending torn pages of a book.
3. Describe how to make each repair using step-by-step directions. Add pictures when needed to make the steps clearer.
4. Write an introduction that tells why it's good to make repairs. Be sure to include safety warnings.

Things That Can Safely Be Fixed

Bicycle chains that are too loose

Books that are losing their bindings

Buttons that have come off

Car upholstery that's beginning to tear

Dolls with broken limbs

Doorbells that don't ring

Doors that don't close snugly

Drawers that stick

Faucets that drip

Flashlights that don't light

Furniture with scratches

Games that have missing pieces or cards

Hinges that squeak

Hoses that leak

Jigsaw puzzles with missing pieces

Locks that stick

Pages that are torn

Pants that need patches

Roller skates with wheels that don't roll smoothly

Screens with holes

Shoes that are scuffed

Tables that wobble

Tires that are flat

Toilets that don't shut off

Toys that don't work

Zippers that are stuck

FOLKLORE

Folklore refers to all sorts of "local" information that people keep in their heads, for example, homemade rules for playing Monopoly.

DIRECTIONS:
1. Choose a group to get information from, for example, family, neighbors, classmates, or club.
2. Make a list of folklore topics. These might include jokes, sayings, legends, jump-rope jingles, ways of preparing foods, beliefs, games, songs, and stories that outsiders may not know about.
3. Ask people to share what they know about some or all of these topics.
4. Organize the material into chapters such as jokes, songs, and so on.
5. Add an introduction that tells about the group whose folklore appears in the book.

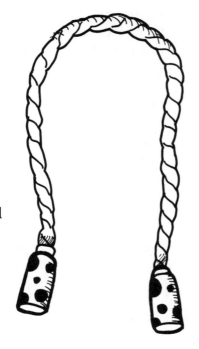

GAME BOOK

While most games have rules, the rules are not always the same everywhere. As people play a game, they often change the rules to make the game fit their particular place.

DIRECTIONS:
1. List favorite games played by family and friends. These can include outdoor games (baseball, Capture the Flag), board games (checkers, chess, Monopoly), word games (Categories, Ghost), and even homemade games.
2. Write an introduction for each game. Explain why the game is worth playing.
3. Give tips for playing each game well or for playing the game in a new way that other people might not have heard about.

FRISBEE TAG

OBJECT OF THE GAME

HISTORICAL NOVEL

While truth may be stranger than fiction, books such as *Wagon Wheels* by Barbara Brenner and *Jack Jouett's Ride* by Gail Haley prove that fiction is sometimes the best way to tell the truth.

DIRECTIONS:
1. Pick a real person who was born long ago. It could be someone famous, for example, Martin Luther King, Jr., or Louisa May Alcott. Or it could be a family member.
2. Learn about that person by reading or by talking to someone who knows about the person.
3. Write a story about that person. Include made-up characters. For example, a character in a story about Abraham Lincoln might feature a made-up character who worked in the kitchen of the White House.
4. Use facts about life during the period in history when the story happened. For example, tell how people traveled or how they dressed.

IFFY INVENTIONS

To find something new under the sun, don't look under the sun. Look into the mind of an inventor.

DIRECTIONS:
1. Make a list of familiar things such as bicycle, book, fork, and television.
2. Pick one of the things and try to imagine how it might be made better, for example, safer or easier to use.
3. Draw a picture of that "new" old thing.
4. Write a few sentences that explain the new twist and why it is a good idea.
5. Create a book of such inventions.

Variation: Make a book about "fixing up" human beings. For example, would eyesight be improved by adding a third eye to the back of the head? Explain why such a change would be useful.

Things That Might Be Improved

Look around the house, school, and town to spot all sorts of items that might be made better. Examples are:

baby carriage

baseball glove

bathtub

braces

comb

doorbell

eyeglasses

Frisbee disk

model airplane

money

newspaper

piano

radio

running shoes

soap

soap dish

teakettle

television

vacuum cleaner

wallet

washing machine

wristwatch

JOB MANUAL

Everybody is an expert about one thing or another. And one joy of knowing how to do something well is teaching the skill to other people.

DIRECTIONS:
1. Choose a complicated household job that can be divided into many smaller jobs.
2. List all the little jobs that make up the big job. For example, if doing the laundry were the big job, the little jobs might include sorting the clothes by color, presoaking stained items, and sewing on loose buttons.
3. On separate pages, describe each little job in detail. Try using pictures to make the steps clearer.
4. Put the steps into proper order.
5. Write an introduction that explains why the big job is important or interesting. If the job is usually thought of as being boring, give tips for making it enjoyable.

Variation: Write a manual for a job that kids might be interested in doing when they grow up. Hint: Read about the job in a book or—even better—gather facts by talking to an adult who actually does the job.

Job Manual Topics

Everyday jobs
baby-sitting
checking the house for safety problems
doing homework
gardening
housecleaning
making a bed
meal preparation
setting the table
shopping
walking the dog
washing the dishes

Adult jobs
actor
animal trainer
artist
assembly-line worker
astronaut
athlete
automobile mechanic
baseball pitcher
bus or cab driver
clown
computer programmer
construction worker
dentist
disc jockey
doctor
farmer
lawyer
magician
musician
park ranger
pilot
plumber
political leader
reporter
salesperson
shop owner
soldier
teacher
travel agent
veterinarian

LETTER BOOK

Most letters are usually written and read one at a time. But sometimes they are collected into books.

DIRECTIONS:
1. Decide which kind of letter book to create. Two choices are:

   A. a pen pal letter book that includes letters between two people
   B. a one-sided letter book that includes only the letters from one writer to many people, for example, *C.S. Lewis' Letters to Children*

2. Choose one or just a few things to write about. Limiting the topics will usually make the book more interesting. For example, the author of one letter book wrote letters to famous people telling them how to handle their problems. In another letter book, pen pals shared their ideas about a science project.
3. Write the letters. Before sending each one, make a copy.
4. Collect all the letters to bind into a book. Add an introduction that tells a little bit about the letter writer or writers.

Variation: Write a book of letters to someone who hasn't been born yet, for example, your grandchild. Tell the person about the different things you do in your present life and what you think the future might be like.

MANNERS MANUAL

Someone called manners "the happy way of doing things that we have to do anyway."

DIRECTIONS:
1. Make a list of activities that can affect other people. Examples include eating, standing in line, and using the library.
2. On separate pages, describe how to do each activity in a way that would please—or at least not disturb—someone who sees or takes part in the activity. Ask other people for their ideas.
3. Use artwork when needed to create a clear picture.
4. When the individual pages are done, write an introduction that explains why it's a good idea for someone to learn good manners.

Variation: Write a funny book of manners that might be used by a certain kind of animal, for example, dogs—if the animals could read.

Topics for a Manners Manual

Bus riding

Classroom behavior (for example, listening to reports)

Combing hair in public

Dog walking

Eating in a restaurant

Eating specific foods

Gum chewing

Introducing people who don't know each other

Job behavior (for example, when baby-sitting)

Library behavior

Meeting people for the first time

Movie theater behavior

Party behavior

Shopping behavior

Talking at the dinner table

Talking in public places (for example, in stores)

Talking on the telephone

Writing thank-you notes

ONE-READER BOOK

Most books are written to be read by lots of people. But a one-reader book is different.

DIRECTIONS:
1. Think of someone who would enjoy a book written just for him or her. It might be a sick relative who needs cheering up, a friend who is moving away, a helpful neighbor, a beginning reader, or a citizen who did a heroic act.
2. Decide what the book will be about. For example, a book for a beginning reader might retell famous fairy tales and, as a surprise, include the child in each one.
3. Write the book. Add an introduction that explains why an entire book was written just for the reader.
4. Give the book to the person for whom it was created.

PARTY BOOK

Everybody loves a well-planned party.

DIRECTIONS:
1. List many kinds of parties, for example, a Valentine's Day party, a surprise party, and so on.
2. On separate pages, give suggestions for making each type of party a success. Include tips on invitations, games, activities, decorations, entertainers, food, costumes, and music.
3. Add pictures drawn from scratch or clipped from magazines.

Variation: Write a book of fantasy parties that might be attended by made-up characters such as the Three Bears or Superman.

PHOTO-CARTOON BOOK

There's an old saying: "You took the words right out of my mouth." Here's a book project that calls for putting words *into* people's mouths.

DIRECTIONS:
1. From unwanted magazines and newspapers, clip out photographs of people and animals. Try to find pictures showing different kinds of activities, for example, a baseball player swinging a bat or a painter painting a picture.
2. Take one of the photos and think up unusual or funny words that the subject might be saying or thinking.
3. Write those words on a piece of paper and cut around the words to make a speech balloon.
4. Paste the speech balloon onto the photograph.
5. Do this with one or two dozen photographs to make a cartoon book.

Variation: Use newspaper photos of famous people to make a current events cartoon book. Each person should be saying something that relates to why the person is in the news.

POPULAR POLLS

People love to know what other people think. No wonder polls are so popular.

DIRECTIONS:
1. Decide if the book will focus on one subject, for example, sports or food—or if many subjects will be included.
2. Brainstorm the categories to include. For example, in a food poll book, some of the lists to include might be: most nutritious cereals, most difficult to eat foods, best things to put into a sandwich, coolest foods to eat in hot weather, and so on.
3. For each topic, ask as many people as possible to give their opinions.
4. List the responses in order from the item getting the most votes to the item getting the least, for example:

Best sandwich filling

chicken	8
turkey	4
peanut butter and jelly	3
sprouts	1

Topics for Polls

Actors and Actresses: best, worst

Animals: beautiful, fast, harmful, ugly, useful

Books: funny, scary, interesting

Dreams: scary, thrilling, unusual

Foods: least and most liked

Games: most fun, most challenging

Jobs: boring, dangerous, interesting

Movies: best, funniest, scariest, worst

Musicians: best, worst

People: bravest, funniest, most creative

Pets: most interesting, most useful

Places: noisiest, prettiest, scariest, ugliest

Records: best to listen to, best to study by

School subjects: most interesting, most difficult

Sports: favorite to play or watch

Vacations: favorite activities

Videos: scariest, best, worst

PRACTICAL PLAYS

It's not easy saying "no" to a door-to-door salesperson. One solution is to prepare for this kind of situation ahead of time.

DIRECTIONS:
1. Make a list of problems such as meeting someone whose name you can't recall or trying to hang up on a persistent telephone salesperson.
2. Write short plays that show how a person might handle these situations.
3. Try out each play by having someone read the lines with you.
4. Write an introduction to the book that explains the value of practicing "tricky talk" before it's needed.

Variation: Write a book of short, just-for-fun plays based on fables, fairy tales, or other short stories.

Practical Play Situations

Admitting to someone that you made a mistake

Asking for information over the telephone

Greeting someone who has just arrived from another planet

Holding a conversation with someone whose name or face you don't remember

Making peace with someone you like after you've had a fight

Ordering a product over the telephone

Refusing to buy something from a door-to-door salesperson

Refusing to buy something from a telephone salesperson

Responding to someone who has blamed you for something you didn't do

Telling someone who disappointed you how you feel

Thanking someone for a gift you don't really like

Turning down a request from a friend

REBUSES

In a rebus story, pictures replace some words or parts of words. Reading a rebus is like figuring out a code.

DIRECTIONS:
1. Write a short story or poem using just words. Skip every other line.
2. Go through the writing looking for words that can be presented as pictures. For example, *be* can be replaced with a picture of a honeybee. The word *need* can be replaced by a picture of a knee followed by a + and then the letter d.
3. Copy over the story or poem with the pictures in place to create the rebus.

I, EYE = 👁

BE, BEE = 🐝

SOCCER = 🧦 +R

CANDY = 🥫 +D

MORE = M+ 🏏

RIDDLES

The word *riddle* comes from an old word that means "to figure out." The word *read* comes from the same old word. Maybe that's why many people who like to read also like to solve riddles.

DIRECTIONS:
1. Make a list of different kinds of riddles. *Hint:* Ask people to suggest types or look through riddle books in the library.
2. Decide what kinds of riddles to include in the book. Some riddle books have just one type, for example, Hink Pinks:

What do you call a writing instrument used by a chicken? Answer: A hen pen.

Other riddle books mix together many kinds of riddles.
3. Write the question part of each riddle on one page and the answer on the back side of the sheet.
4. For an extra clue, add a picture to the question page.

WHERE DO CATTLE GET THEIR NEWS?

FROM NEWS BULL-ETINS!

Four Kinds of Riddles

New-word Riddles

The answer to this kind of riddle includes a made-up word that sounds almost like a regular word. Just a letter or two is changed:

> What's the title of a book about a boy who wants to climb a nasty vine? Answer: Jack and the Meanstalk.

> What do you call a fancy car for a kitten who is a movie star? Answer: A Catillac.

Rhyming Riddles

The answer to this kind of riddle—known as a Hink Pink—is a pair of words that rhyme:

> What would you call a piece of wood used by a feline in a game of baseball? Answer: A cat bat.

> What would you call a tax on the creature that makes honey? Answer: A bee fee.

If the answer has two syllables, the riddle is called a Hinky Pinky:

> What do you call a fuel that's made out of roses? Answer: Flower power.

Sound-alike Riddles

The answer to this kind of riddle includes a pair of words (homonyms) that sound alike but have different meanings:

> What do you do when you take a vacation by the ocean? Answer: You *see* the *sea*.

> What do you call the story about the part of a dog that wags? Answer: The Tale of a Tail.

Traditional Riddles

The answer to this kind of riddle is simply a clever answer to a tricky question:

> What kind of bird is like a letter? Answer: A jaybird.

> What has ten heads and ten tails? Answer: Ten pennies.

> How can you make seven even? Answer: Take away the first letter.

SEQUELS

"The End" doesn't have to be THE END. Some stories can go on and on and on.

DIRECTIONS:
1. Pick a familiar story such as "The Three Little Pigs" or "The Wizard of Oz."
2. Write a new adventure that picks up where the old one ended. For example, the Wizard who lived in Oz might visit Kansas. Or the three bears might explore Goldilocks's house.
3. At the end of the story, write a note that invites readers to write their own sequels.

Variation: Instead of writing a new adventure of the same sort that was in the old story, the new story could be very different. For example, it might make fun of the old one.

SMELLY BOOK

Years ago, a movie was made using "smello-vision." When someone was shown in a garden, the audience got a whiff of flowers. The same idea can work as a book.

DIRECTIONS:
1. Think up a list of smells that you can capture on a piece of cotton. For example, soak the cotton in orange juice to make the smell of oranges.
2. Write a story that has scenes that include the smells on your list. Put each scene on a separate page.
3. Prepare each smelly cotton ball and then place it in a resealable plastic bag. Attach the bag to the page with the matching words or to a facing page.
4. Include an introduction that tells readers about the smells and when to sniff them.

Sample Smells

after-shave lotion

almond extract

apples (use apple juice)

catsup

chewing gum

chocolate (mix cocoa and water)

coffee

cola

flower petals

garlic

grass

onions

oranges (use orange juice)

peanut butter

perfume

room deodorizer

soap

tea

toothpaste

vanilla

vinegar

STUFFED BOOK

Most books are made up of words. Only a few also contain things, but those that do can be a lot of fun to read and even more fun to make.

DIRECTIONS:
1. Think up a mystery story in which all the clues are small, thin objects, for example, a comb, a toothpick, a piece of cloth, a piece of yarn.
2. Write the story in a way that when a clue comes up, the reader will want to look closely at it.
3. Place each clue in a plastic, resealable sandwich bag.
4. Write the finished words on the left-hand page of each spread. Tape the bag with the clue to the right-hand page.
5. Add an introduction that tells the reader to remove each clue and study it, and then return the clue to its bag.

Variation: Instead of a mystery story, the book can be about a school subject. For example, a stuffed science book might present different types of leaves, cloth, paper, seeds, and so on.

TONGUE TWISTERS

Tongue twisters have been around for thousands of years. But there's still room for new ones—especially twisters that no one has ever heard before.

DIRECTIONS:
1. List the names of friends, classmates, teachers, and family members.
2. Pick one of the names. List words that start with the same sound as the person's name. For example, if Charla is a friend, list words such as chicken, choice, chip, chocolate, and chance. A good dictionary will come in handy.
3. Now write a tongue twister that uses some of the words in a way that makes sense . . . sort of. For example: "Charla's choice is chicken and chocolate chips."
4. Repeat the tongue twister several times quickly and see if it's difficult to say.
5. Create a tongue twister for each person.

Variation: Make a tongue twister book using characters from stories, movies, fairy tales, and so on.

TRAVEL BOOK

Every place is interesting if a person knows what to look for. The job of the travel writer is to make sure the reader doesn't miss anything important.

DIRECTIONS:
1. Make a list of interesting places. The places might be real, for example, the school, the zoo, a museum. Or they might be imaginary places visited only in books, for example, Oz or Alice's Wonderland.
2. Choose one of the places and list all of the places within it. For example, in the school there are classrooms, the library, the office, the cafeteria, the playground, and so on.
3. Write about each of the parts on a separate page. Tell a visitor things to look for. For interest, add one or a few drawings.
4. Draw a map or picture that shows all the parts of the main location. Use this artwork as the first page in the travel book.

ON THIS SPOT, PAMELA BORTON BROKE HER LEG IN 1989. PAMELA WAS

VIDEO DIRECTORY

The VCR is an amazing machine, but it is useful only if the tapes it plays are good. A video directory can help viewers find worthwhile programs.

DIRECTIONS:
1. Make a list of film categories such as action, comedy, dance, drama, horror, musical, romance, science fiction, and western.
2. Make a list of favorite films that fit into each category. Ask family and friends to suggest titles.
3. Describe what each film is about and add a sentence or two that explains what makes the film special.
4. Make up a rating system for the films. For example, four thumbs up might mean "best film in its group" while four thumbs down might mean "worst film."
5. Rate the films.
6. Add an introduction that gives tips for how to enjoy a film at home.

WELCOMING WORDS

Nearly one out of every four families moves each year. Being a new kid in the neighborhood or at school can be confusing and even scary. Some friendly words can help.

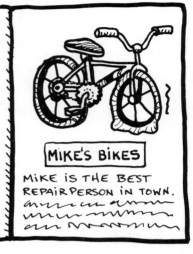

DIRECTIONS:
1. List kinds of information that might be helpful to a kid who is new to town, for example, the name of a neighbor who is home after school in case of an emergency.
2. Write up the information. Include a map plus useful details such as phone numbers and addresses.
3. Add an introduction that tells what's special about the town.
4. Keep a master copy of the book for making duplicates.
5. Give a copy to each new family.

People, Places, and Things For the Newcomer

Barber shop/beauty parlor

Bicycle repair shop

Dangerous animals (dogs that bite)

Dangerous intersections

Dentist

Doctor

Library

Little League

Movie theaters

Music teachers

Natural disasters to prepare for (earthquakes, tornados)

Playgrounds

Sandwich shop with tastiest food

School principal

Videotape store with best collection

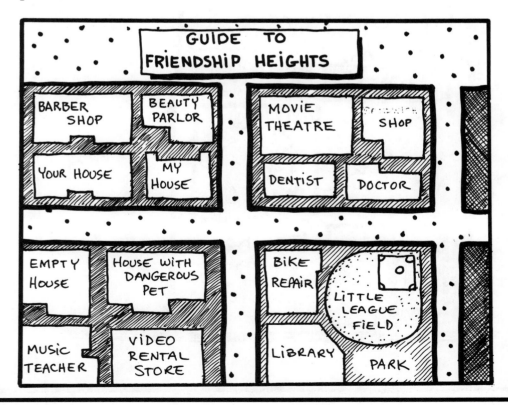

WHO'S WHO WHO NEVER WERE

There are books about the lives of musicians, actors, ball players, inventors, and other famous people. But what about "people" who never really lived except in books, movies, and other worlds of the imagination?

DIRECTIONS:
1. Make a list of imaginary characters from books, movies, TV, and comics.
2. Write a short biography about each "person." Describe what the character looks like and what makes him or her so special. Include information about his or her adventures.
3. Write an introduction that explains why real people should pay attention to imaginary people.

Famous Imaginary Characters

Alice (of Wonderland)
Amelia Bedelia
Babar
Bambi
Big Bad Wolf
Black Beauty
Boy who cried "Wolf"
Br'er Rabbit
Bugs Bunny
Charlie Brown
Charlotte (from *Charlotte's Web*)
Cinderella
Clementine
Curious George
Doctor Dolittle
Donald Duck
Dorothy (of *The Wizard of Oz*)
Eloise
Gilly Hopkins
Gulliver
Hiawatha
Horton
Huckleberry Finn
Humpty Dumpty
Jack (who climbed the beanstalk)
King Kong
Lassie
Little Miss Muffet

Little Red Riding Hood
Long John Silver
Lucy
Madeline
Mary Poppins
Max (of *Where The Wild Things Are*)
Mickey Mouse
Mowgli
Mrs. Piggle-Wiggle
Nancy Drew
Paddington Bear
Peter Pan
Peter Rabbit
Ping
Pinocchio
Ramona
Riki-Tiki-Tavi
Roger Rabbit
Rumpelstiltskin
Snoopy
Snow White
Stuart Little
Superman
Three Little Pigs
Thumbelina
Tom Sawyer
Uncle Remus
Willy Wonka
Winnie the Pooh

WHY? WHY? WHY?

Babies know what they're doing when they repeat the word "Why?" Asking questions is one of the best ways to get smart about the world.

DIRECTIONS:
1. List as many questions as possible about puzzling things. For example: "Why are words reversed when seen in a mirror?" or "Why do cats meow and dogs bark?"
2. Pick the most interesting questions and find the answers in books or by talking to experts.
3. Put each question and its answer on one page. Add illustrations.
4. Write an introduction that explains why questions are so important.

WORD EXPLOSION STORY

Like an explosion, a single word sometimes shoots out many different meanings and uses. This kind of word can star in an unusual kind of story.

DIRECTIONS:

1. Pick a word that is used in many phrases, compound words, song lyrics, sayings, and titles. An example is *top.*

2. Make a list of as many uses as possible, for example:

top-notch	top prize
tiptop shape	top billing
top it off	"Sitting on top of the world"
tippy top	top of the morning
make it to the top	top dog
top 40	top heavy
top-flight	spinning top
top hat	*Top Gun*

3. Write a story that includes as many of the uses as possible. It's OK to use different forms of the word—top, topping, topped.

> I live on the top floor of an apartment building. Everything is top drawer—a great view, a balcony, and a big kitchen. To top it off, there's a wood floor that is perfect for spinning a top. I happen to be the top top spinner in the country.
>
> One day, while I was listening to a top-40 radio station . . .

4. Add pictures that help show many of the word's different meanings.

61

Words with Many Uses

air (fresh air, airplane, hot air, air conditioning, etc.)

back (back seat, talk back, quarterback, backup, seat back, horseback, etc.)

break (give me a break, take a break, breakfast, breakaway, daybreak, etc.)

drop (eyedropper, drop everything, drop in the bucket, dropcloth, drip drop, etc.)

eye (eye of the needle, eyeball, eye of the storm, black-eyed pea, evil eye, etc.)

heart (heartbeat, heartbreak, heartache, heart of lettuce, ace of hearts, etc.)

in (into, ins and outs, inside, indeed, way in, back in, etc.)

light (lighthouse, limelight, lightweight, relight, etc.)

line (line of poetry, give someone a line, clothesline, etc.)

play (play ball, play money, child's play, play a song, etc.)

red (red light, red lips, red roses, redhead, etc.)

water (water over the dam, in hot water, water wheel, etc.)

WORD HISTORIES

Why is a tall building called a skyscraper? And why is a hit out of the ballpark called a home run? Every word has a story, which is called the word's etymology.

DIRECTIONS:

1. Brainstorm a list of words whose stories—called word origins—will be given in the book. The book can tell the stories of all sorts of words, or it can focus on a specific kind of word, for example:
- football words (huddle, touchdown, fumble, offside, end zone, quarterback)
- medical words (flu, asthma, cold)
- names (why is a classmate named Bill Smith called "Bill" rather than "Joe" or "Sam"?)
- product words (Coke, Pepsi, 7-Up, Dr. Pepper)
- places (why is Tombstone, Arizona, called "Tombstone"?)

2. Try to learn the story behind each word on the list. This may be done by reading dictionaries and word origin books. Another possibility is talking to people, or writing letters, for example, to companies asking how their products got to be called what they are.

3. Write each story on a separate page.

4. Add pictures that help explain some of the word origins.

Words That Come from People or Places

begonia

boysenberry

braille

cardigan

Danish pastry

denim

diesel

doily

Ferris wheel

frankfurter

graham cracker

guillotine

hamburger

jeans

leotard

Levi's

nicotine

Pennsylvania

pickle

sandwich

saxophone

sequoia

sideburns

teddy bear

tuxedo

volt

RESOURCES

Creating a Classroom Publishing Company

Writing well is hard work. But there is a natural reward, namely, publishing. This doesn't mean getting a big contract from a New York company. Publishing means sharing the written word. It involves everything from illustrating to binding to advertising. But at the core is sharing ideas, facts, experiences, and visions.

To produce and distribute a book is not a frill. This key literacy activity is as important to students as it is to professional authors. Publishing teaches beginners the crucial idea that people write *to be read.* The process lets students experience the bond that links writer and reader in the search for truth and delight.

Beyond its contribution to the writing program, classroom publishing is a giant source of self-esteem. Just watch young authors' faces as they read their latest works.

Of course, establishing a classroom publishing company takes some effort. But you don't have to do it all yourself—and you shouldn't. Your job is to create a framework that will invite and enable students to handle most of the work. This way, in addition to getting books into circulation, the company will provide students with opportunities for:

- collaboration
- decision making
- taking responsibility
- problem solving

1. Help students learn about publishing.

After telling your class that you would like to launch a publishing company, it's a good idea to make sure they know what such an enterprise is all about.

Publishers turn out all sorts of word products such as books, magazines, newspapers, greeting cards, calendars, and posters. Bring in examples and discuss the elements: typography, design, art, paper, color, and so on.

If possible, read aloud and discuss the informative *How a Book Is Made,* written and illustrated by Aliki (Crowell, New York, 1986).

Invite a local publisher to talk to your class about the nature of the business. You might also have students do reports on the publishing business.

Later, list the jobs that will have to be done if your company will have success. These might include:

- writing the books
- illustrating manuscripts
- typesetting or lettering
- binding
- advertising
- distributing

2. Name the company.

Brainstorm a list of possibilities. The following categories may help stimulate ideas:

Characters:	"Snoopy, Ink"
Literary qualities:	"Can't-put-them-down Books"
Objects:	"See-saw Stories"
Places, literary:	"Oz Publishing"
Places, real:	"Washington School Writers"

To avoid having the name selection become a popularity contest, you can have each student vote for two favorites on the list, then put the top three names in a hat and choose the "winner" by a random drawing.

Have a group of students make a banner or flag to fly over your publishing center. Announce the company's grand opening with a student-made poster attached to your classroom door.

3. Gather the materials.

Have students bring in the items that will go into book production. Here is a "starter" list:

- cardboard (lightweight) for book covers
- clip art books
- crayons and markers
- fabric remnants and felt
- hammer and nails (for creating binding holes)
- paper: plain, construction, tracing, wrapping
- paper punch
- pencils
- plastic tape
- rubber cement and glue
- rulers
- scissors
- shelf paper (self-sticking, transparent)
- wallpaper sample books
- wood panel (size of page in biggest book)
- yarn

Books were invented long before electricity, so you don't need a computer and printer. However, having a word-processing setup will enable your students to vary type size and style for a variety of dramatic effects.

4. Set up the publishing area.

The following questions may help you and your students develop a functional and comfortable place:

- Is the area colorful and inviting?
- Is there room for both independent and collaborative work?
- Are containers for storing materials clearly labeled?
- Are rules and procedures posted for easy review?
- Is there a location for record folders listing students' individual projects and contributions to class books?
- Is there a display area for completed books?

5. Give authorship options.

The classroom publishing company can be used by students to create individually authored books or class books which contain writing from everyone in the room . . . including the teacher.

6. Encourage students to explore all sorts of writing.

Students often prefer to publish just one type of book—stories, jokes, whatever. Like most people, they feel more comfortable with what they already know.

There are, however, strong reasons for encouraging students to attempt all sorts of writing. Doing so will broaden their interest in reading. Variety also enables students to develop a wider range of writing skills.

As you monitor your students' efforts, you might make sure that during the year they try at least one project that fits into the following categories. Because specific projects may fit into more than one group, the samples are included merely to help clarify the categories.

Exposition: using facts and ideas to explain things
    Advice Book
    Almanac
    Atlas

Instruction: teaching skills
    Fix-it Book
    Party Book

Narration: telling real or fictional stories
    Autobiography
    Diary
    Smelly Book

Word play
    Riddles
    Tongue Twisters

7. Teach the conventions of each format.

It's not enough to ask students to write a certain kind of piece—or even encourage them to choose on their own. Every type of writing—story, letter, pun, whatever—presents unique problems. Rather than have students flounder—which often drains away enthusiasm and may also result in immature work—many teachers use an instructional process that includes:

- Reading models by professionals, by students, and—sometimes—by the teacher.

- Discussing the key features of the given type of work. Giving students step-by-step directions or planning sheets can help them focus their creativity. Naturally, your young writers should have the freedom to experiment and even to invent original forms.

- Helping students establish the purpose and the audience for the piece.

- Showing students how to develop their ideas by brain storming, researching, or interacting with a partner.

- Making sure that students understand that a first draft is a rough draft. The motto here is "Guess and Go." The aim is to get down ideas without concern for spelling and punctuation. It's OK to cross out, start over, fill in, write out of order. Revising/editing will come later.

8. Help students polish their work.

After manuscripts have been drafted, they must be edited. (Some people prefer the word "revised.") Whatever the term, this step involves looking for and solving two kinds of writing problems: content and mechanics.

Content editing comes first. This refers to anything that can be detected by listening to the piece read aloud: facts, organization, formatting, word choice, and sentence structure. Mechanics editing deals with spelling and punctuation.

As far as possible, students—and not the teacher—should do the editing. This will involve self-editing (a solo activity) and peer editing (a collaborative editing). For each type of editing, students will, of course, need guidance from the teacher.

Self-editing

To efficiently encourage self-editing, create a "First Reader Editing Folder" for each assignment. The specific content items to be checked are listed on the inside left page. The mechanics items are listed on the right page.

These folders probably should be kept in the publishing area. After drafting a manuscript, a student can retrieve the appropriate folder and use it as a framework for editing.

It helps if the teacher models the use of the folder the first time, so that students will know how to relate the checklist to their individual manuscripts.

Peer editing

After writers have checked—and changed—their drafts, they are ready to test their manuscripts with trial readers. Because no one is born knowing how to give encouraging and useful feedback, the teacher must carefully structure this kind of interaction. This can be done by giving editors specific directions for providing feedback. For example, the directions might tell writers to begin the editing conference by reading their work aloud while the peer editor simply listens.

The peer editing guidelines might also include specific questions that the editor should think about before giving feedback. For example, if the manuscript is a storybook, content questions might include:

- Are the characters clearly described?
- Is the setting clearly described?
- Does the dialogue move the story along?
- Does the story build to a climax?

It takes time to formulate editing questions for each format, but once prepared they can be used again and again.

Note: As with teaching self-editing, modeling an editing conference will help clarify this activity.

Teacher editing

Self-editing and peer editing cannot entirely replace teacher feedback. While, with practice, students will eventually produce stronger, cleaner manuscripts, the teacher will still be needed to ensure that the finished books will be of the highest quality. But creating a better product isn't the only—or even the main—point. By using the same criteria that the students used, the teacher will reinforce the fundamental concepts of editing.

9. Show students how to design their books.

Depending on the format, individual books and class books alike should include the following elements:

- cover
- title page
- about-the-author page
- dedication
- table of contents
- body of the book (words and pictures)
- check-out pocket so that students can take the book home to read to their families and friends

The best way to clarify these items is through the study of models. For example, students might bring in examples of books with favorite covers. The class could then analyze what makes a good cover—art, color, grabby title, dramatic phrase, and so on.

When it comes to laying out the pages, encourage students to experiment with the size and style of type used for headlines, subheads, captions, and initial letters. Design work also includes decisions about the size and placement of illustrations and borders.

As part of the design process, publishers often make a "dummy copy." While this "model" will be rough, it should contain the exact number of pages that will be found in the final book.

At this point, final art can be produced. Illustrations can take many forms: original drawings, copied drawings, clip art, original photos, copied photos, charts, maps, and computer art.

10. Teach procedures for binding the books.

Go over the types of bookbinding available in your publishing area. Typical options are:

- Stapling: This is the simplest method. Staple the pages and the cloth cover along the edge. Then cover the edge with plastic tape.

- Rings or yarn: After hole-punching the pages and the cardboard covers, use rings or yarn to join the parts.

- Machine spiral binding: This requires a GBC binding machine and plastic end binders.

- Ready-made binders: This approach is especially useful for class books.

- Hand-stitched binding: This method is more complicated, but it is preferred for books meant to become part of the permanent collection of a room, school, or city library.

STAPLES

Use posters to display clear, step-by-step directions for each method that students will be using. Also, train two or three students to be "binding specialists" for each project. This delegation of authority fosters independence and problem solving. It also lifts a bit of the burden from the overtaxed teacher.

Hint: For detailed descriptions of each binding method, see *Book Factory* (Monday Morning Books, 1988).

11. Find readers.

Each book that the classroom publishing company brings out should have an intended audience. But extending the list of readers can prove motivating. Try some of these:

- other classrooms—students and teachers
- parents
- relatives
- school staff: principal, secretary, nurse
- citizens at large—by getting local librarians and bookstore owners to take copies
- doctors' and dentists' offices

Don't overlook publicity. Arrange for displays of the books in public places such as shop windows, the board of education, and city hall.

For more drama, hold a publishing party for a major classroom book or for a shelf of individually produced books. Invite the local media to come, see, and then report on the fact that literacy is alive and well in your school.

12. Evaluate the results.

It's satisfying to send a book into the world of readers. But don't stop there. After the excitement of publication has passed, ask your young authors to reflect on the books they have produced. A simple journal writing activity might involve answering questions such as:

- What do you like best about the book?
- If you could change one thing about the book, what would it be . . . and why?
- What is the most important thing you learned by publishing this book?
- What is the next book you'd like to publish?

A final thought: If your students enjoy turning manuscripts into books, you might encourage them to offer a publication service to other classes, especially to children in the younger grades. Helping other people enter the world of arts and letters is a joyful, memorable experience.

Desktop Publishing Comes to School

In desktop publishing, a computer is used for two purposes: *word processing:* typing, revising, and printing text; and *graphics:* creating pictures, borders, and other visual effects.

Professionals use computers to produce books, magazines, newspapers, brochures, calendars, and other printed products. But does this innovation have value for students? That question was recently answered by a room full of genuine experts—St. Louis fifth graders who had used computers regularly for several years:

> "Writing on a computer is better and neater than handwriting, and erasing doesn't show!"

> "It's easier to make designs on the computer because you can color using FILL [an electronic option] instead of spending hours coloring with markers and crayons. Your fingers don't ache!"

> "You acquire keyboarding and word processing skills for the future."

> "Keyboarding becomes faster than writing by hand."

Word Processing

Electronic writing's biggest plus is that it encourages revision and editing. Tap a few keys or move a "mouse" (a kind of electronic marker) and words are quickly erased or moved or inserted.

Another benefit: the text is highly legible. This makes it easier for writers to spot wrong words, repetitions, omissions, and related problems.

Because mistakes can be fixed without affecting the surrounding text, effort goes into conceptual matters rather than copying.

The computer also helps with spelling. An electronic "spelling checker" identifies possible errors and may offer suggested changes. The machine does not, however, correct mistakes. That responsibility still belongs to the writer.

Spelling checkers do have their limitations. They can't find homonym errors ("too" instead of "to"), nor can they catch typographical substitutions ("he" for "the"). Thus, students must still invest time checking their work carefully.

On a more creative level, word processors enable students to vary typography—which can lead to interesting possibilities for titles and for body text. There are options for font (style) and size.

More sophisticated programs such as PageMaker and Publish It! allow writers to arrange type in columns—perfect for producing classroom or school newspapers and magazines.

A

Graphics

Most graphics programs offer options such as:

copy, which duplicates an image

cut and paste, which moves part of an image to a new location

erase, which erases specific areas of a drawing

fill, which completes a closed figure with a solid color or pattern (see Illustrations A, B, C)

shapes, which draws ready-made geometric figures

spray paint, which draws with a spray effect

undo, which cancels the last operation and thus corrects a mistake

zoom, which magnifies a specific working area in order to add or edit details

B

C

Teaching Tips

You don't have to be a computer "hacker" to help students with desktop publishing. However, basic familiarity with the computer and the software is essential. This means such things as being able to:

- tighten loose wire connections and solve other minor mechanical problems
- adjust the intensity of the monitor
- unjam printer paper
- control the major operations of the software

None of this is harder than driving a car or operating a food processor. To gain the needed expertise you can read manuals, experiment, take a class, work with a friend, or allow students to share their often impressive knowledge. The main block may be the uncomfortable feeling most of us experience when exploring new territory. Be patient and you will soon be able to make the apparatus do almost everything you ask of it.

Scheduling Suggestions

Because you may be unavailable for consultation when help is needed, it makes sense to prepare students to work independently.

Try teaching the entire group a certain operation. Support this instruction by placing how-to posters near the equipment. Another idea is to write a manual for the students' level. (This takes work at first, but once you have the booklet you can use it forever.)

The best resource may be student experts who, with a bit of training, can help their classmates.

Materials

Computerized publishing requires hardware and software.

The basic hardware setup consists of:

- a computer with a monitor (screen)
- a printer—with color ribbons, if possible

Experienced computer users are often partial to one company or another—Apple, Atari, Commodore, IBM, Radio Shack, and so on. While most brands offer roughly the same features at about the same quality level, some software may not run on all machines.

Software products are packaged instructions (programs recorded on disks) which turn a computer into a smart typewriter, drawing tool, or other device. Scores of word processing and graphics programs are on the market. The items listed below—most of which come in versions for the major brands of computers—are among the best available. Several of these items were used to produce the examples shown in this section.

Software for Desktop Publishing

Bank Street Writer (Broderbund Software)
Dazzle Draw (Broderbund Software)
Koala Painter with Koalapad Touch Table (Koala
    Technologies)
Logo Writer (Logo Computer Systems Inc.)
PageMaker (Aldus)
Paintworks Plus (Mediagenic)
The Print Shop, The Print Shop Companion, The Print
    Shop Graphics Library (Broderbund Software)
Publish It! (Timeworks, Inc.)

by Jayne I. Hanlin

Jayne I. Hanlin teaches fifth grade at Spoede School in
Ladue, Missouri.

Computer graphics by Margo Heger and Michelle Dutra

Book List

Presenting models is one of the best ways to teach any form of writing, including bookmaking. The idea is to focus on the structure, not the content. By putting their own material into the form, children will create original books using the same forms that experienced writers rely on.

The books listed here are mainly for elementary students. In some cases we have found no models written for students. However, even then, presenting adult examples—for example, the *World Almanac*—can help young writers understand the task you have set for them.

ABC Book for Big Kids

Q Is for Duck by Mary Elting and Michael Folsom (Clarion, 1980)

Advice Book

Playing It Smart by Tova Navarra (Barrons, 1989)

Almanac

The Old Farmers' Almanac (Yankee, Inc.)
Polish American Almanac edited by Ellen Blaustein (Cemrel, St. Louis)

Anthology

Packet of Poems: Poems About Food collected by Jill Bennett (Oxford, 1982)

Atlas

National Geographic's Picture Atlas of Our Fifty States (National Geographic, 1978)

Autobiography

Self Portrait by Trina Hyman (Harper & Row, 1981)

Code Book

Codes and Secret Writing by Howard Zim (Scholastic, 1975)

Diary

On the Frontier with Mr. Audubon by Barbara Brenner (Coward, 1977)

Family Future

My Family 'Tis of Thee: The Ellis Island Workbook by Ira Wolfman (Workman, 1989)

Folklore

Whim-Wham Book collected by Duncan Emrich (Four Winds Press, 1975)
Family Words by Paul Dickson (Addison-Wesley, 1988)

Game Book

Games by Imogene Forte (Incentive, 1983)
A Book of Puzzlements by Herbert Kohl (Schocken, 1981)
Super-Colossal Book of Puzzles, Tricks & Games by Sheila Barry (Sterling, 1978)

Historical Novel

Ben and Me by Robert Lawson (Little, Brown, 1934)
Courage of Sarah Noble by Alice Dalgliesch (Scribner, 1954)
Why Don't You Get a Horse, Sam Adams? by Jean Fritz (Coward, McCann & Geoghegan, 1974)

Iffy Inventions

How to Be an Inventor by Harvey Weiss (Crowell, 1980)
Steven Caney's Invention Book (Workman, 1985)
Weird and Wacky Inventions by Jim Murphy (Crown, 1978)

Letter Book

Letters to Children by C. S. Lewis (Macmillan, 1985)

Manners Manual

Telephone Time by Ellen Weiss (Random House, 1986)

What Do You Say, Dear?/What Do You Do, Dear? by Sesyle Joslin (Harper & Row, 1958)

Party Book

Confetti: The kids' make-it-yourself, do-it-yourself party book by Phyllis and Noel Fiarotta (Workman, 1978)

Rebuses

Bunny Rabbit Rebus by David A. Adler (Puffin, 1983)

Riddles

A Mad Red Hen and Other Riddles by Joseph Low (Greenwillow, 1977)
1800 Riddles, Enigmas, and Conundrums by Darin Hindman (Dover, 1963)
Hink Pink Book by Marilyn Burns (Little, Brown, 1981)

Stuffed Book

Who Killed Robert Prentice? by Dennis Wheatley (Rutledge Press, 1980)

Tongue Twisters

Tongue Twisters and Tricky Tanglers by Duncan Emrich (Scholastic, 1975)

Who's Who Who Never Were

Who's Who in Children's Books by Margery Fisher (Holt, 1975)

Word Explosion Story

Follow the Line by Demi (Holt, Rinehart, 1981)

Word Histories

American Talk by J. L. Dillard (Vintage, 1976)
Guppies in Tuxedos: Funny Eponyms by Marvin Terban (Clarion, 1988)